FIELD PRESENCE:

It's Not Enough Just to Play the Game

FIELD PRESENCE:

It's Not Enough Just to Play the Game

Wes Booker

and

E m i l y   M i n g l e d o r f f

I am grateful to God for His love, His salvation through Jesus Christ and His faithfulness in my life.

To God be the Glory, forever! Amen.

I dedicate this book to my mom, Ezelma Booker, my children (and sweet granddaughter), my sister, Georgetta "June" Sullivan, and my family and friends whose love and devotion continue to encourage me to pursue my dreams. *I love you.*

Thank you, educators, coaches and players who continue to inspire me to *do more, influence more and be more than I ever dreamed.*

Table of Contents

Introduction

FOREWARD

Wes Booker has field presence and you recognize that from the moment you meet him. He has a servant's heart and it's evident in the way he lives his life and gives back to his community. Through hard work and with a smile on his face, Wes has achieved much both on and off the field. For all of us who have played football or other competitive sports and understand the way it helped prepare us for the game of life, Wes will remind you of that special coach you had teaching, motivating, and encouraging you to be your best. For all readers, Wes will challenge you to do more than just play the game.

Congressman Bruce Westerman

About the Author

George Wesley Booker II, 2017 Class member of the Arkansas Sports Hall of Fame (1991 NAIA National Football Champions) grew up in White Hall, Arkansas. Only three years old when his father died, Wes's mother focused on good morals and Christian principles he honors to this day. After graduating from White Hall High School, Wes played football for the University of Central Arkansas Bears, where he graduated with a Bachelor's degree in Business Administration.

Wes moved back to White Hall and quickly became part of the fabric of his community. He founded, through a God-given vision, a professional minor league football team for late-bloomers: the Central Arkansas Rhinos. As head coach and general manager, he used the team as a conduit to offer good players an opportunity to play longer and to be seen by the arena league and the NFL.

In 2002, within months of starting with Farm Bureau Insurance Company, Wes broke a myriad of life insurance records. He won the National Sales Achievement Award two years in a row and the National Multiline Sales Award, six years in a row, among other prestigious awards.

At the same time, Wes was officiating football. After officiating at the high school level, he was invited to officiate several bowl games, and has since worked his way up as an official in the Southeastern Conference (SEC). In 2013, Wes received the honor of being inducted into the White Hall Sports Hall of Fame.

Continuing in the SEC, Wes is also the owner and CEO of his own insurance agency, creator and director of his own officiating camp, and a motivational speaker. He serves on various boards and volunteers in whatever capacity he is needed, including mentoring at an elementary school in his hometown.

From player to coach to SEC Football Official, and from employee to employer, Wes leads with a servant's heart and a football player's passion. Join him as he details his struggle to overcome failure, his journey to influence others, and his rise to success in his motivational book *Field Presence: It's Not Enough Just to Play the Game*.

Introduction:

You've never tried anything new if you've never failed.

You hear about the success stories all the time; the people who achieved fame by being the best in their field. They are loved and praised, considered heroes in their professions. But did you know some of those household names started out as failures?

Take, for instance:

Albert Einstein. *He couldn't keep a job.*

Abraham Lincoln. *He ran for public office 7 times and lost before being elected President of the United States.*

Walt Disney. *He was fired from a Missouri newspaper for not being creative enough.*

Each failed – some many times – but not one of them allowed their failure to define them. Each went on to accomplish more than anyone dreamed. But how?

From third grade on, my goal and ambition in life was to be a running back in the National Football League (NFL). I played college and professional minor league ball and tried out for different teams. Ultimately, I failed at making an NFL team. But that failure didn't make me give up my dream. In what follows, I discuss how my dreams evolved from disappointment and how I continue working to make those dreams into reality. You can, too!

As you journey through this book, utilize the playbook provided at the end of each chapter. The questions are meant to help you determine how to get where you want to be.

I hope you are encouraged and motivated to do more, to be more, and to influence more than you thought was possible.

Special thanks to my football officiating crews, supervisors, and officials
over the years for the opportunity
to work with the *best*.

CHAPTER 1

WHAT IS FIELD PRESENCE

YOU CAN'T FALL IF YOU DON'T CLIMB, BUT THERE'S NO JOY IN LIVING YOUR WHOLE LIFE ON THE GROUND.

"You can't fall if you don't climb, but there's no joy
in living your whole life on the ground."
- Author Unknown

Field presence is generally a sports term. It's actually a *skill* in sports. It is the physical or mental ability for a player to see and respond at just the right time, despite the many possible distractions. The action of a player with field presence is preemptive – a reflex. It just happens. Not by chance, mind you. It occurs due to the awareness and impulse of a player so familiar with the game that he or she can see a play before it happens.

Field presence is the moment a football player comes out of nowhere and intercepts the ball. The instant a pass-rusher gets a glimpse of a small hole and runs through to sack the quarterback... The second a basketball player steals the ball and passes it to his teammate down the court to score... Somehow these players sense the next play, see how to bring the rest of the team into it and rally their team to achieve the goal.

A player with field presence is consistently in control, leads with confidence, has the respect of his or her peers and perseveres. Coaches, teammates, opposing teams, and fans are keenly aware when a player with field presence takes his or her position for the game because their presence changes everything. The momentum changes, the amount of excitement changes – for everyone! Field presence compels teammates to listen, draws the attention of first-class coaches and emboldens professional teams to spend millions of dollars for players who possess it.

I understand field presence because I've used it most of my life as a football player as well as a coach. I'm aware how its use on the field leads to endless opportunities and jaw-dropping achievements. Yet for me, field presence is more than that. It is a tool I've applied to many areas of my *life*.

As with most of life's tools, field presence is easier to explain than to impart. In fact, I know individuals who have the *traits* of field presence, yet the real skill eludes them. There is nothing wrong with these people, per se - - they are overachievers with lofty goals who pursue getting to the top of their field. They are multi-taskers, leaders and influencers. They have vision, strategy, motivation and perseverance; all things individuals with field presence possess.

However, having field presence is more than all that; more than marking traits off a list and playing a good game. It is especially more if you want to apply it to your life.

The first thing to realize is that outside the realm of sports there are additional criteria required to have field presence.

- **What are the criteria?**
- **How do I apply field presence to aspects of my life?**
- **What do I gain from applying it to my life?**

We are taking this journey to answer those questions.

As we begin, let's compare and contrast field presence in sports and field presence in life:

- Both impact teams on the field and at work.
- Both carry weight psychologically because having field presence is apparent to everyone around.
- *But they are derived from different places.* Field presence as applied to sports comes from a competitive drive to excel and achieve. *The field presence you apply to life comes from who you are and what you're about. It stems*

from your character and your purpose. **Character charts your direction and purpose drives your determination.**

The Heart of Character

Character may not need to be defined, but I want to be clear what I mean in the context of field presence.

Character is similar to the heart of a person. It is the vessel through which everything must flow and is pumped to the extending areas of a person's life. Like blood flows into and out of the heart, all our "stuff" flows into and out of character. Information flows through, actions and reactions flow through, discipline flows through and motivation flows through. If our character is damaged (or non-existent), some part of us suffers just as if our heart were damaged.

To take it a little further, there are dimensions, or traits, of character. Like the chambers of a heart, each trait has its own role and fits its function perfectly. The dimensions of character – motivation, empathy and integrity – must work together consistently for character to be genuine, much like the chambers of the heart must work together for a person to be healthy.

To have true character, all the dimensions of character must be present to guide a person's actions. They provide a framework – a structure of motives, habits and morals, which are consistent despite circumstances, setbacks and disappointments.

Let's take a break from all the information I'm throwing out there to unpack what I'm saying and connect it to field presence:

1. Can a person have character but not field presence? Yes. Many people have character but don't understand how to utilize it to impact their game.

2. Can a person have field presence without character? Sure. Being involved in a sport does not require character.

3. Can a person without character have field presence in sports *and* in business dealings, personal relationships and community? No. Character – a moral structure – is required to apply field presence to those areas of life.

The bottom line is that a person with character does the hard things when he or she can get by with doing easy things. He or she puts forth more effort than is required to do a good job. He or she respects rules and structure and views them as a system in which he or she can maneuver and work with success. He or she owns mistakes and admits problems as they arise. He or she is humble and appreciative to others.

Let's put a face on it. Do you know anyone with the type of character I'm describing? Might someone with character be a mentor in your life? Or perhaps, a hero?

My Hero Has More Character than Your Hero

Everyone has a hero, right? A hero is basically a mentor or a person to look up to. It might be a mom or dad, or perhaps an entertainer. Something about that particular person is so impressive that folks are inspired to duplicate his or her persona, attitudes or abilities.

In theory, a hero sets the standard for achievement or what it takes to get there. My hero makes that theory a reality. He had incredible field presence on the football field; he was a successful coach. But his field presence off the field was just as impressive. Both exemplified his heart and his character.

Tony Dungy was the head coach of the NFL Tampa Bay Buccaneers from 1996 to 2001 and the Indianapolis Colts from 2002 to 2008. He was legendary for his strategic coaching skills and his keen grasp of football. Throughout his career, win after win, he proved himself to be the best. However, he wasn't just known for his wins on the football field.

Many people recognize the name Tony Dungy because he did things other coaches were afraid to do – things many traditional coaches perceived as weak and irrelevant to the actual game of football. For instance, his players remember his coaching style to be unique because he stayed calm and didn't yell a lot. His explanation for being able to coach without all the negativity? The Golden Rule: "Do unto others as you want done to you." He tried to coach the way he'd want to be coached; he wouldn't like being yelled at, so what good came from yelling at his players?

That kind of respect and thoughtfulness of others was on the field and off the field. Time after time, and day after day, Dungy allowed his interactions with people to be navigated by his character. He was as much about caring for others as he was about winning football games.

No matter when or where your interaction with him, Dungy was going to treat you with dignity and respect. It's just who he was.

It's easy to have good character when life is good. You know, when you're winning Super Bowl games and smiling for cameras day in and day out... But what happens to character when life gets tough? Does it stay "good" on bad days? Or does character turn with the tide?

In my opinion, if ever there is an appropriate time to show bad character, it is in the midst of sorrow and grief. During difficult times, a person has a good excuse to have a bad attitude. Many times I offer grace to people whose character flaws show during crisis. After all, nobody is perfect. Everybody has "bad character" days, right? But as it turns out, those with authentic character don't buy into that way of thinking. Individuals with good character might even call overlooking someone's character flaws in the midst of crisis, "cheap grace." People with authentic character don't allow circumstances to change how they react to the world. That's what makes them stand out.

The public got a glimpse of Dungy in the worst of circumstances as we watched him live through the devastation of his eldest son's suicide. James, Dungy's 18 year old son, tragically killed himself in

December of 2005. Tony Dungy and his family, as well as his team, the Indianapolis Colts, were devastated by the loss.

Dungy could've cursed God; he could've ranted and raged about what caused depression in his son; he could've found someone or something to blame. He could've allowed bitterness to set in and harden his heart. But he didn't.

Somehow, Dungy's reaction to his personal tragedy remained consistent. He handled his heartache the same way he handled his happiness- with humility and graciousness.

At the 19th annual Athletes in Action Super Bowl breakfast in Detroit, his first speaking engagement since his son's funeral, Dungy shared his grief with a packed ballroom of former NFL football players and coaches. He spoke of his sadness and heartache. But he also spoke of how positive things came from the loss of his son, including two people who received the gift of sight from his son's donated corneas.

"If God had talked to me before James' death and said his death would have helped all these people, it would have saved them and healed their sins, but I would have to take your son, I would have said no, I can't do that."

21

"But God had the same choice 2,000 years ago with His Son, Jesus Christ, and it paved the way for you and me to have eternal life. That's the benefit I got, that's the benefit James got and that's the benefit you can get if you accept Jesus into your heart today as your Savior."

Tony Dungy was humble yet unwavering. His character was such that his go-to was to acknowledge God's presence, even in his pain, reminding anyone listening that God knew pain, first hand. Then, he went further to say that because God sacrificed His Son, Jesus, James got the benefit of eternal life in heaven, along with anyone else who accepted it. Then he invited those who would, to accept it!

Wow! I am overcome with emotion every time I share Dungy's story. Though his circumstances might have affected his happiness at the time, he didn't allow those circumstances to alter who he was and how he acted.

How did Dungy manage to find hope and peace in such tragedy? His grief traveled the same moral framework as everything else. A framework which was not haphazardly put together. It was foundational. Everything else was built on it, from it and through it.

Authentic character is required to do what we are trying to do here. We want to apply field presence to life. Tony Dungy is my hero because he is a living example of doing it. It's possible. Therefore, I have no excuses.

Character becomes evident as its traits become consistent despite circumstances, setbacks and disappointments.

Purpose Drives the Ball

Our first chapter continues with laying the foundation for field presence – the kind you can apply to your life. We discussed character. It is the "how to" get the ball in play. Now we look at purpose. Purpose is the "why" the ball is in play.

Why am I playing football (or enter your job here)? *Why* is this worth my time? *Why* does this really matter? *Why* should I care? *Why* should I try? *Why*?

What Really Matters is the Why?

Colonel Joshua Lawrence Chamberlain was tasked with defending the far left flank of the Union Army at Little Big Top near Gettysburg, Pennsylvania in 1863. Things looked bleak. His soldiers were weary and had little ammunition. To make matters worse, on the trip from Maryland to Pennsylvania, he had acquired 120 insubordinate soldiers. (The men had an axe to grind with army administration over enlistment.) Realizing the potential for mutiny, Col. Chamberlain was instructed to shoot any man who harried havoc in his unit.

The task before him seemed impossible. Chamberlain had to rally this group of angry, resentful soldiers to action, and quickly. If the Confederates got through the line his men were ordered to hold, the Union Army would be surrounded

There he was – an exhausted Union colonel leading a group of restless, unpaid mutineers – ordering them to put their lives on the line for a bloodbath of a war, with nothing but empty gun barrels. It was a hard sell, to say the least.

Yet, he was successful!

On Colonel Chamberlain's orders, all but six of his men held the line. Then they charged the Confederates, without ammunition! Chamberlain's men armed their rifles with bayonets and raced into combat. That event was an astounding display of courage and passion!

24

How did he do it? What did he say to get those disgruntled soldiers to follow his orders? It must have been something powerful!

That it was. Col. Joshua Lawrence Chamberlain rallied his group of weary, derelict soldiers with his reminder of their purpose – *why* they should fight.

I love this story. I find hope in that Chamberlain inspired the best of men who found themselves in the worst of circumstances. Chamberlain didn't panic or give up. Nor did he *force* his soldiers to do anything they did not want to do. He didn't shoot his men for deserting. He didn't threaten them or shame them for their anger and ranting about their unjust enlistment.

Though their issues with the army were valid, Chamberlain refused to debate them.   He realized it was more divisive, and ultimately, a waste of precious time to bicker.

Instead, Chamberlain reminded his soldiers what they were fighting for – not for money, not for power and not for bragging rights! He persuaded his men that nothing mattered more than the reasons they initially joined the war: to win the freedom of fellow Americans and to save the unity of their young country. At that point, their combined purpose inspired them to lay aside whatever personal issues they had and, ultimately, to fight for a higher cause.

Purpose should do the same for you and me. It should be the driving force behind everything we do. The reason? **Only when our purpose is significant will the battles ahead be worth fighting.**

In sports, field presence may or may not be built on character and purpose. The two are not required to have good presence on the field. Nonetheless, hopefully you understand that *life* field presence is different.

The criteria for *life* field presence is unwavering character and definitive purpose. With unwavering character and definitive purpose, quitting is not an option, leaving is not an option, running away is not an option, hiding is not an option, surrendering is not an option. Character won't put up with it and purpose won't allow it. When we have character and purpose, we are driven by more than mere will power; like Dungy and Chamberlain, we are driven by passion.

We will discuss what field presence looks like, and how to acquire it, in the chapters ahead.

PLAYBOOK: Field Presence

1. Define field presence in your own words.

2. The foundation for field presence is made up of character and purpose. Why?

3. Tony Dungy is my heroic figure. Who is your character hero and why?

4. What is the meaning of "character is an inner structure of morals?"

5. Why is character and purpose more than will power?

CHAPTER 2

LOOK LIKE A PRO

MAKE THE FIRST HIT COUNT

Let's discover how to have field presence. Principle #1: Look like a pro. Or as **Coach Porter Taylor said, "Make the first hit count!"**

True story: James sent his resume to Alan. Alan, impressed with the resume, decided to interview James. As Alan readied his office for the interview, he found himself thinking, "This guy is great. I hope he accepts my offer."

However, as soon as James walked into the interview, Alan did a complete about-face. Why? James's resume was excellent. He was qualified for the job and could take the position within the month. Yet after meeting him, Alan hesitated.

James was friendly, knew the business, was responsive to questions, was well-spoken and carried himself with confidence. Yet none of that mattered; he didn't get the job due to his presentation in person.

James showed up to his interview in skinny jeans, an untucked collared shirt, wearing flip flops. I'll write that again for emphasis: he wore flip flops to his interview! What was he thinking?

Well, I know what Alan was thinking. He thought meeting James was a waste of time because James didn't represent, in person, the professional he presented on his resume.

First impressions matter. Anyone who tells you otherwise is wrong. People make assumptions about you through their perception of you. As a matter of fact, once an impression is made, it is difficult to change it. We become attached to our original ideas of people, regardless if those initial impressions are correct.

Don't Judge About... Judging

Before getting on a soap box about "judging a book by its cover," you might as well admit, it's something all of us do. We make assumptions about others based on our perception of them. It is only human. The adage "You'll never get a second chance to make a first impression," is true. If we are savvy, we will be honest with ourselves and use that to our advantage.

Presentation Sends the Message

I play many roles in my life. Each requires something a little different for me to make a good impression. I own a business, have a

30

family, I officiate and do some public speaking. Yet, I don't have to say a word to communicate which role I'm playing at any given moment. The message is clear by my presentation. I wear a different outfit for officiating than I wear for playing golf. I wear a suit when I'm working with educators or lecturing at speaking engagements. You get the idea. But that's not all.

If I stay in shape, stay well groomed, conduct myself in a suitable manner, speak with integrity and make proper eye contact, I radiate positively, no matter which industry I work. Anything less is not an impression I want to leave.

Regardless your profession, you are
making a first impression. Make it a good one.

Make a Statement

When I meet someone for the first time, I want my impression to be loud and clear: "I am worth your time, your effort and your trust. I am qualified and will be the best at whatever I do. Remember me because I will make a difference."

Likewise, if you want to have field presence, your presentation should be in harmony with the message you are attempting to project. For instance, if I'm on the field expected to defend my quarterback, I'm not going to have unicorns bouncing through daisies with hearts painted on my facemask or my mouth guard. I'm not saying there's anything wrong with unicorns. But make no mistake about it. I'm not trying to project a silly, playful image as I block the defensive players who are trying to sack my quarterback. No! I want to look like I'm going to cause massive pain if they mess up my offense. That's part of my job!

Credibility, stability, professionalism, education, and respect begin with your presentation. If you want to be perceived as someone who is detached, lazy and irresponsible, roll out of bed and go to a job interview. If you desire to be perceived as put together, reliable, sensible, educated and trustworthy, take some time to shower, dress professionally and speak with credibility. Even more, walk with confidence, shake hands firmly and make eye contact. Remember, regardless of your profession, you are making a first impression. Make it count!

Dress the Part

Dressing the part might be difficult for some of my younger colleagues to appreciate, but it is worth mentioning. I realize the current generation lives in a period of dressing casual for everything. School is casual attire. Church is casual attire. The office is casual attire. Even businesses have adopted more casual attire. (Friday has been deemed "casual" day for many businesses, these days.)

Although we live in a "casual" world, there is still something to be said about dressing for success. First and foremost, when you dress professionally, you are more likely to be treated as a professional. This reality is especially important for those who work in financial services. People are much more likely to trust a professionally-dressed financial planner with their hard-earned money, compared to someone who arrives in cargo pants and a golf shirt. Credibility is innately given to the individual dressed to impress. And that's not all.

Dress for Your Next Position

"Dress for the position you want, not for the position you have."

Jada was hired as a receptionist when she really desired to land a better paying executive assistant position at the local office of an international company. Remembering the advice her father gave her when she was applying for jobs as a teenager, she intentionally dressed differently than the other receptionists. While her peers wore khaki pants and trendy shirts or sweaters, Jada put forth the effort to dress more like an executive, wearing stylish suits. To Jada's surprise, she was the first one considered for a promotion and was moved straight to the executive floor. Now Jada repeats her father's words to her kids as they are going into the workforce. Why? Because she believes her father was right. Her appearance as a professional helped her move to a more professional position.

You don't have to spend significant money and have the latest fashion at your fingertips to have field presence. However, recognize that in every situation you are making an impression, sending a message and marketing yourself. Make sure the message you send is that you are the best and the most capable at whatever you do, whatever your profession!

PLAYBOOK: Look Like a Pro

1. List the things you hope people notice upon their first
   impression of you.

2. Do you do the necessary things to project that impression?

3. Are you dressing for your next position? Why or why not?

4. Summarize how first impressions impact field presence at work.

CHAPTER 3

COMMAND RESPECT

SILENCE CAN NEVER BE MIS-QUOTED

"Silence can never be misquoted."

- Wes Booker

Your next step is to *command* respect.

Respect is a heavy word. The Bible uses it. Teachers use it. Gangs use it. My mama uses it! There's even a song about it sung by Aretha Franklin - R.E.S.P.E.C.T! To make things more complicated, everyone wants it. Why?

Essentially, respect suggests value. When you respect someone, you value *who* they are, what they *think* or *say* and the *decisions* they make. Consequently, if you want to have field presence, you're going to need respect.

There are two ways a person can get respect: the good way and the bad way. People can command it or demand it. And there is definitely a difference.

For our purposes here, we will define these terms as follows.

- A person who commands respect is admired and valued for who he/she is *within*. This person has no need to take action against people who don't appear to value them because his/her value doesn't rely on

37

someone else's opinion. He/she has respect for him/herself, and it shows in how he/she carries him/herself and treats others on the field and off the field.

- A person who demands respect is one who desires control and uses fear to prove his/her worth or value by using punitive tactics to keep people looking up to him/her. Put in simple terms, when a person who **demands** respect doesn't receive it, there is a price to pay.

When a person who demands respect doesn't receive it, there is a price to pay.

Earn It

Earning respect is no easy task. It requires diligence and consistency. It only occurs as you allow people to see you work hard, do your best, respect others and exceed expectations, over and over again.

Consider Peyton Manning. No matter your favorite team, if Peyton Manning walked into the room, you would stop what you were doing and stand in line to shake his hand. He would probably have the entire room on their feet in no time. Immediate respect. Why?

Because, as fans, we saw his hard work and talent in action, and he exceeded our expectations! He was a heck of a quarterback and a great team leader. Manning doesn't have to say a word or lift a finger to gain respect. He commands it. It automatically happens when he shows up. But only because he worked for it.

Worried yet? Don't be worried. For those of us who cannot prove our worth on the football field like Manning, here are some tips to get going in the right direction.

Dress for Success

I realize I'm repeating myself here, but it is important enough to repeat: dress for success. When you walk into a room, look like you are someone who is...*someone*. Dress appropriately and perhaps even a little above how everyone else is dressed. Take pride in dressing for success and carry yourself as such because dressing for success sends the message that you mean business.

Make a Strong First Impression

On the heels of the advice to dress for success is another repeat: Make a strong first impression. Studies show that people will make a judgment about you within 30 seconds of meeting you. Make those 30 seconds work for you!

- Shake hands firmly. A limp handshake is the sign of someone who lacks confidence.

- Smile with confidence. There is no need to look angry to command respect. Respect does not mean "unapproachable." The key to commanding respect is to treat people like you value them as fellow human beings. That's difficult to convey if you're frowning and distracted.

Be Aware of Body Language

Nonverbal behavior speaks volumes! Therefore, consider what you're saying without speaking. I might sound like your mother here, but indulge me - it's for your own good!

- Stand straight. Good posture conveys self-confidence and excitement. Don't lean. Don't droop. Don't put your elbows on the table with your head in your hands. Correct posture is straight with your shoulders rolled back.

- Be present. Avoid fidgeting and looking at your cell phone. Body language (e.g., shaking your foot, tapping your fingers, biting your nails, twitching your nose, touching your neck and twirling your hair) can distract and convey uneasiness. I have a friend who touches his beard while he talks to me, every other word. I find myself distracted because I want to know whether his beard is mere facial hair or some kind of an animal he's petting, attached to his face. It drives me crazy. Commanding respect means communicating a sense of control when you walk into a room.

Please notice I didn't say, "having control." A commanding presence doesn't always *have* control. One who commands respect is in control of themselves and their space – not everyone else.

Be a Role Model

A person who commands respect understands that people are watching how they carry themselves and how they interact with others. Therefore, they take seriously their reputation, the things they say and the things they do.

41

If you are my age or older you may recall the "Be like Mike" Gatorade commercials in the early nineties. There was a jingle about *being like* Michael Jordan as pictures of him flashed across the screen. In each picture, he was surrounded by kids, parents, players and Gatorade, while playing basketball and having good, clean fun.

Gatorade's genius marketers didn't make up that phrase simply because it rhymed. Michael Jordan was the ultimate role model at that time. They intentionally chose him because he was proven to be good enough in basketball, and in life, to imitate. Parents approved. Teachers approved. Athletes approved. Even non-athletes respected Michael Jordan!

We can't all be role models like Mike. But we *can* be role models that Mike would be proud of! So what are *you* doing to be a role model?

Give your audience a reason to love you.

I can't imagine my school years without role models, especially after losing my father when I was three.

My mom did a great job raising me! I can't give her enough credit for her heart, drive and determination. And yet I also needed *something* else outside of my home – something to push me; to passionately pursue. For me, that something else was football. Ironically, however, football and other sports were not as important as the relationships I made while playing them. I'm not just referring to the friends I made. Those relationships were great. Rather, I'm talking about the mentoring relationships I made – with the *coaches*.

I spent hours every week with my coaches. They taught me self-respect, confidence and humility. They taught me how to be a humble winner and a good loser, how to play my part and how to work hard. They taught me how to keep going when I didn't think I could. They taught me about *life*. They played a major role in shaping me. It's my turn to do that for others.

For this reason, I donate some of my free time to a local elementary school by mentoring young boys about how to become successful young men. Many of the things I say to them are echoed in these pages.

I also pride myself on the fact that my business serves unsung heroes like teachers and other educators. Those public servants make a difference in our world so it's important to attempt to make a difference in theirs.

I hope if, or when, my role models see me, they recognize the investment they made is paying it forward, two-fold.

To have field presence, find a way to be a positive role model. Invest in your community, love people and be humble.

Be Excellent at Something

"Whatever you are, be a good one."
— Abraham Lincoln

Whatever your hobby, job or profession, find something, and be excellent at it! Be the "go to" for an issue, an event or a phenomenon for which you are passionate. Pick anything. Having expertise at *something* makes it easy to have confident conversations with anyone. It's always easier to respect someone who is confident.

Revere not Fear

We started this chapter discussing commanding respect versus demanding respect and why respect matters. Let's close with some examples.

An extreme example of one who demanded respect is Adolf Hitler. Actually, he's not only an extreme example; he's the poster child for it. Hitler was infamous for *demanding* respect - motivating through fear and control. Though he was charismatic and likeable at the beginning of his leadership, it ended up that he controlled people by exerting authority and/or bullying them. If you fell into a category that Hitler thought little of you would be killed. Millions of people were murdered because they fell into one of his "hate" categories like religion, skin color, mental capacity, etc. The only way to stay alive, let alone thrive under Hitler's reign was to be what he valued and to follow his orders.

Hitler needed to be feared (respected) to accomplish his ultimate goal: world domination. He demanded it because his power stemmed only from his grip on those he terrorized. When he lost control, he lost respect. When he lost respect, everything he built crumbled.

In contrast, commanding respect creates interest, trust, dialogue, room for growth and a regard for others. The poster child for that? Mother Teresa —the complete opposite of Hitler.

Mother Teresa motivated people to do good by loving others. She commanded respect due to *her* respect for human life at all phases and in all situations. Being in her presence could bring a grown man to tears out of reverence for her.

In short, *demanding* respect is not part of field presence, nor is it a way to acquire it. Rather, field presence goes hand-in-hand with *commanding* respect by the virtue of being able to walk into a room, or on to a field, and have people anticipate *positive* things because you are near. Commanding respect is desired and appreciated. Most importantly, in order to apply field presence to your life, **people don't need to fear you; they need to revere you.** Therefore, commanding respect is not just a better option, it's your only option.

PLAYBOOK: Command Respect

1. What is the difference between commanding respect and demanding respect?

2. Name three people in your life who exemplify commanding respect.

3. How does becoming a role model assist you in commanding respect?

4. What are ways you can be a role model or give back to your community?

CHAPTER 4

FAKE IT 'TIL YOU MAKE IT

IF YOU AIN'T CHEATING YOU AIN'T TRYING

You've heard the phrase "Fake it 'til you make it." Have you ever asked yourself, "What, exactly, is *it*?" For our purposes here, "it" refers to confidence. That's right. Fake confidence until you *are* confident.

I don't always feel confident. However, I never show inadequate confidence, whether I have it or not. Why? Because I know **confidence has a profound effect upon performance.**

As a matter of fact, confidence is much bigger than many of us believe. The views we hold about ourselves impact what happens to us. Furthermore, it's not limited to just one area of our life. It plays a key role in creating healthy connections, making and achieving goals in your professional life and maintaining focus. The bottom line is that we *need* it – especially if we desire to have strong field presence.

However, not everyone grasps their need for it, let alone how to achieve it. Don't worry. Let's go over some easy ways to muster confidence, even if it's not your natural state of mind.

Step 1: Claim the Truth

First of all, let's not forget who we are! There are countless times we lack self-confidence simply because we look at ourselves outside of who God is and His love for us. When we don't acknowledge that we are God's children made in His image, we tend to become self-deprecating. We dwell on our faults and insecurities rather than reminding ourselves of the truth that God's children are His masterpiece.

On my worst days- on days I believe I don't deserve to walk this wonderful journey called life - I remember this: God loved us enough to send His Son to save us so He obviously believed we have value. And due to the resurrection of Jesus, we have a bright future with Him for eternity. Therefore, since I was made and then saved, I *must* be loved.

Claim the reality that you are God's child and you are loved. You were wonderfully made. Don't underestimate what claiming that can do for your confidence!

Step 2: Practice, Practice, Practice

Self-confidence is summed up in one word: self-fulfilling. If you think it, you can be it. Therefore, self-confidence can be built with perspective and practice.   Though it sounds like I'm oversimplifying things, stay with me.

You've heard of self-fulfilling prophecy - if you think you are going to fail, the chances of you failing are better than the chances of you succeeding. Therefore, rather than thinking about failure, think about success. If you think you will succeed, you are more likely to do things to ensure success. When I hear people say, "I *knew* I was going to mess that up," I want to say, "What would've happened if you *knew* you were going to do it perfectly?" That's the idea – think about doing it right, not messing up.

Confidence can actually be the turning point of your thoughts into actions. *Think* positively; *act* positively.

Confidence is not Arrogance

It is important to understand that self-confidence is not the same as arrogance. Just as confidence plays a positive role in how you relate to others, arrogance is negative. The difference is internal, but visibly, very external. A person with confidence believes in him/herself without having to prove it to a room full of people. A person with arrogance feels the need to have a room of people validate his/her greatness without believing it him/herself.

Self-confidence draws people near and builds them up; arrogance aggravates people because it is meant to make them feel inferior.

"No one can make you feel inferior without your consent."
- Eleanor Roosevelt

Here's the bottom line - though self-confidence seems difficult to achieve, it is easy to fake. That's why "Fake it 'til you make it" is key advice for individuals who want to be successful. Use the self-fulfilling prophecy approach because it works. But until self-confidence is a permanent part of your demeanor, here are some other basic ways to fake it.

Good posture

Good posture is one of the best things you can do for exuding confidence. Plus, your whole body benefits! Not only does it help you appear self-assured and calm, it helps your body function properly by opening airways and giving everything room to work - your organs and tissues need space to work at full capacity. The key is to stand straight, with head high and shoulders back.

Eye contact

It is no secret that the amount of eye contact one makes indicates a lot. After all, it's claimed that "The eyes are the window to the soul." Eye contact establishes a valuable connection to the people with whom you interact, and it is key to appearing confident. Consistent eye contact is interpreted as a sign of trustworthiness. Inconsistent eye contact is interpreted as a sign of dishonesty.

However, before you get carried away and stare down the host of the next event you attend, understand that eye contact also establishes dominance and can be interpreted as threatening. Therefore, it's important to find the proper balance between confidence and creepy!

Don't fidget

Again, body language discloses more about you than anything you say verbally. Hence, fidgeting is interpreted as a sign of nervousness and/or anxiety as it distracts from any other message you are trying to send. Fidgeting includes playing with your hair, biting your nails, tapping your fingers, shaking your leg or foot, nodding frequently, shifting your weight from one foot to the other and overusing hand gestures.

The most effective way to find out if you fidget, or how often you fidget, is to get help from a friend. Ask him/her to watch your interaction around others and to call your attention to any fidgeting as you do it. You might be surprised to find how often you are perceived to be nervous simply because you have the inability to be still. Or perhaps you'll be surprised at how nervous you are, seeing as you *can't* be still. Or, maybe you'll be told you caress your beard like it's a pet. Regardless, you'll be doing yourself a favor because fidgeting is distracting, as well as annoying.

There is POWER in Poses

Ever feel the urge to randomly hit a superhero pose? Oh, c'mon. Perhaps when you nailed a presentation, saved a failing account or figured out that math problem for your third grader? Perhaps when the other team went for a touchdown to push ahead during the last seconds of a game, and you intercepted the ball? Let's be honest, friends. Everyone, at some point in time, has wanted to strike a pose like Superman – even adults.

Well, I have good news! Superhero poses are not just for kids any more. Studies by Social Psychologist, Amy Cuddy, show that striking a power pose for two minutes creates a response in your body which helps boost confidence. More testosterone, the dominance hormone, is produced during and following these poses – which results in lower cortisol levels (stress fighting hormone).

What are power poses? Amy Cuddy did a TED Talk in 2012 and explained the poses and the scientific evidence behind them. They are body positions which are perceived as confident, versus body positions which make you appear weak and insecure. The poses are all about releasing your body and taking up more space, much like primates do. The idea is to look larger to achieve dominance.

There are many poses from which to choose, but the ones which stood out to me were the superhero poses. Think Wonder

Woman and Superman – feet flat on the floor, legs shoulder-width apart, hands on hips, shoulders rolled back and head held high. Striking and holding this pose for two minutes brings back great childhood memories, as well as boosts confidence. Win-win!

Put It in Context

I admit that most of the time, the advice "Fake it 'til you make it" seems trite, to say the least. And the advice to strike superhero poses sounds...well, crazy. Yet in the context of confidence, it's the best advice you can receive. Self-confidence goes a long way toward adding to your credibility.

Have confidence in faking confidence. It's one more way to apply field presence to your life. Plus, it could take you to the next level where you might need to know how to fake it anyway! As **Coach Steve Edwards says, "If you ain't cheatin', you ain't tryin'!"**

PLAYBOOK: Fake It 'til you make it

1. Why is important to appear self-confident?

2. What is the difference between self-confidence and arrogance?

3. Name some ways to gain confidence.

4. What does "faking it" mean in terms of confidence?

5. List some ways to "Fake it 'til you make it."

CHAPTER 5

TEAM WORK FOR THE DREAM TO WORK

HE WHO KNOWS OTHERS IS WISE, HE WHO KNOWS HIMSELF IS ENLIGHTENED

"The strength of the team is each individual member. The strength of each individual member is the team."
- Phil Jackson

If you're going to have field presence in life, it's a team effort. Whether you're leading the team or playing alongside the team, field presence requires shared goals and working with others to achieve them.

Phil Jackson is a former NBA basketball coach who holds the NBA record for winning the most combined championships. He was named one of the 10 greatest coaches in NBA history. But perhaps most impressive was his knack for creating cohesive teams made up of individual superstar athletes. With players like Michael Jordan, Shaquille O'Neal, Kobe Bryant and Scottie Pippen, he worked with the most talented ballers the world has ever seen. Jackson was unique in that he realized these mega players didn't need more work-outs, more defensive drills or more offensive plays. They needed to merge egos and play as a team. Sure, they each had their own incredible value, but if they learned to work together, they could be unstoppable.

Michael Jordan must have agreed. One of his most famous quotes sums up his coach's teamwork mentality: "Talent wins games, but teamwork and intelligence win championships." And that they did. Jackson's teams won the most championships of any other NBA coach in history, and he's the only coach who won multiple championships with more than one team.

There is No 'I' in Team

When you dissect what *makes* a great team, you find it's exactly what Phil Jackson said. It's "the strength of the team's individual members." It's how they've worked and cultivated their position, their muscle control, their perseverance, their stamina. They play their position, they're always ready for the next challenge, they consistently put forth the effort and they give more each time they play. They're often proud and pushing for more, always wanting to be the best they can be. The better they become, the harder they work. They are the guys and gals you want on your team.

Unfortunately, however, there is a tendency for the best individual athletes to become proud and narcissistic, which creates a culture of self-centeredness and haughty pride to the detriment of their team. Again, that's why Jackson was such a successful coach – he was able to coach egos. Many times coaching egos is possible. But not always.

I had a player on my team who thought he was incredible. Indeed, he was! However, he thought he was so good that he needn't listen to the coaching staff or come to practice. Because he did things his own way, I had to remove him from the team. The unfortunate truth is that the only thing that stopped him from playing and excelling in the sport was his ego. It kept him from being a team player.

I had a similar experience with an assistant coach. As Head Coach, I set the direction for the team. This particular assistant wanted the team to go in a different direction, so he consistently tried to convince the players to follow his agenda rather than the teams. His divisiveness became a tumor, spreading poison through the entire team. He eventually lost his job because having his own agenda created such dissention.

There is no room on any team for *that* type of player. As a matter of fact, there is no room for that type of player in business, or even in life. Those individuals kill motivation in others and sabotage the stability of the team/organization. **The most valuable players don't push to be the best on the team. They work to make the team the best**.

What I've learned is that an effective coach - - a successful leader - - desires individual members of a team who are driven and focused on being their best while developing strength with and for their team. What's more, the best players do it realizing that when they come together *with their team,* they achieve more than they could without the team.

American Cartoonist, Tom Wilson, said it beautifully when he said, "Some of us are more capable than many of us. But none of us is as capable as all of us."

I play both coach and player roles in my personal life and career. But it's through teamwork that I accomplish the most. Accepting the role as a member of a team makes me a better person and pushes me beyond what I can do for myself.

The environment of a team facilitates growth. Don't neglect being part of a team, and if you're part of a team, don't neglect your role to make the dream work.

Communication is Key

The fundamental element of all the coaching in the world is wrapped in one word: *communication*. The first thing any coach should do is to make team members aware of the goal. He/she sets the direction of the team by casting the vision so the play can be set into motion. The way to keep the play going the right direction is accomplished by having a solid team and empowering the players to complete the play, making the goal, or vision, a reality.

Relationship

It takes a special skill to cast a vision the team believes in enough to individually sacrifice whatever it takes to accomplish it.

I understand my job as a coach is to cast the vision and rally the troops to accomplish that vision. But now I've figured out what separates a good coach from a great coach.

A good coach does some basic things and does them well. A great coach does the same basic things but does the process more efficiently, and with one key element: relationship. Take "relationship" in the context of casting vision, for instance.

Vision

Anyone can cast a vision. But it takes a special skill to cast a vision that the team believes in enough to individually sacrifice whatever it takes to accomplish the vision. Team vision is only possible with the ability to create a team mindset centered on a shared goal.

Though it sounds easy, it is difficult because you, as the coach, must allow the team to assist in creating the vision without losing your own vision. This is accomplished only when there is good and inclusive rapport among everyone involved.

Many organizations avoid using this *team* vision approach, utilizing the old fashioned top-down process in which the leader makes decisions and then tries to convince the team to go along with it. Sometimes that approach works. However, I've found that generally, players don't want to be used to **reach** a goal; they want to help **determine** the goal.

The heart of a team wants to be involved in setting the direction and the path. A great coach realizes this and provides opportunities for everyone's voice to be heard and taken into consideration, whilst staying focused and consistent about how to move the vision into reality.

This vision-casting process continues as long as the vision is clear to the entire team. Everyone should state the vision and the reason the vision exists. This creates an opportunity for buy-in as well as making expectations clear.

Buy-in is especially important because members of a team generally appreciate a coach who doesn't presume to tell them what to care about. Concern occurs naturally to them because a culture of discourse has been established and their feedback is valued.

The next part of the process is where many coaches fail. It's the action part. Sometimes a vision is cast and agreed upon, but how to get there is never discussed.

A great coach offers the route to attaining the vision by empowering the team to improve their individual roles and become the most effective they can be. The best way to do that is to have a positive attitude and become a *family*.

Faith, Family, and Football

Remember the old adage, "People do not care how much you know 'til they know how much you care?" It's true. "Faith, family and football" was the motto of my semi-pro team, the Rhinos. It wasn't a saying I pulled out of a helmet one day. It was the truth. I was proof. I had lived it.

Faith was first. My mama taught me that. Her passionate love for God influenced me and shaped me more than anyone or anything. Then, since my father died when I was three years old, my football coaches and teams became a very big part of my world. In Chapter 3, I mentioned how my coaches became my role models. I'd even go as far as to say my coaches became father figures, encouraging and disciplining me. The players on the team became my brothers. We were *family*, and our family happened to play *football*.

Due to the love, motivation and kindness I experienced on my childhood football teams, as well as through high school and college, I understood how important it was to recreate that atmosphere when I became a coach. In doing so, the players on my teams understood how much I cared about them and they played their heart out for me and for their family – the rest of the team.

Ultimately, my goal was to be the best role model of how players should live life on the field and off the field. I spent most of my time trying to be the best I could be to bring out the best in each of them, much like my coaches did throughout my football years. Through my coaches' example, I went above and beyond for my "family". I loved my players, and they knew it. Perhaps most importantly, I prayed with the kids before and after practice, realizing that I might be the only Christian presence in their life.

As soon as we established that we were family, my players did not want to disappoint me or the team. Their lives were enriched by their experience, and so was mine.

The Individual

"A boat doesn't go forward if each one is rowing his own way."
- Swahili Proverb

We've discussed how the coach inspires and leads a team toward a shared vision. But what is the role of the individual members on the team?

First, every player needs to know where their boat is heading so they know which way to row. Second, they need to row together. In other words, a team member's job is to embrace the team vision and with others, make it a reality.

I'm no theologian. But I can't help but consider the example of the Trinity in the context of the Christian faith. In the Trinity, God the Father, the Son and the Holy Spirit operate as one team (three in one). They work to accomplish one goal.

God the Father is the coach. He casts the vision of Kingdom life through the life, death and resurrection of His Son, Jesus Christ.

Christ illustrates God's unconditional love because He was the sacrifice sent by the Father to reconcile humanity. He was on the ground, in the game. He made the plays. Ultimately, He conquered death through the resurrection.

Through the guidance of the Holy Spirit in us, the goal is accomplished.

The ultimate goal? Salvation.

Over-simplified? Sure. But diluted or not, that's how teams are supposed to function — everyone on the team working together toward the common goal.

A person with field presence knows the value of the team as well as each individual on the team. Understanding this dynamic, he/she can help or even shift the focus to make the team the most effective it can be.

"He who knows others is wise. He who knows himself is enlightened."

- Lao Tzu

Team field presence is a game-changer. No matter where you find yourself – as the coach, an individual, or a teammate – in a game or in life - working together is key to achieving your goals.

PLAYBOOK: Teamwork

1. In what areas do you see yourself as a coach?

2. Define your mission as a coach, then as a teammate.

3. What's your vision as a coach? As a teammate?

5. Teams motivate us, lead us, push us and embrace us. Everyone should *have* a team in their personal lives. Some people call it having a personal board of directors, or executive committee of sorts. Let's call it your offense. Take a moment now and build your team. Who do you want on your team and what position do they play in your life/business/organization?

CHAPTER 6

GET OFF THE BENCH

GET TO THE LINE

Do you want to make a difference?

Get off the bench!

Do you want to win those awards at work?

Get off the bench!

Do you want others to work as hard as you do?

Get off the bench!

In a football game, you can't have field presence unless you get off the bench. The same is true in life.

Most of getting off the bench is based on intentionality, effort and timing before you get the call. As a matter of fact, the intentionality and effort you put into building your position before you get to the field will directly impact whether you ever make it off the bench. Other things are basic – things you just have to do, and do unfailingly! Here is a sample of basic things that every successful person needs to do consistently:

- Get up early each day.
- Get enough sleep.
- Go to bed on time.

- Take care of your body through exercise and diet.

Seems simple, right? Then why do so many people fail at these basic things? Because they don't flex their *discipline* muscles enough.

If you fall into this category, don't worry. There is good news. Discipline can be built using a couple of tools: diligence and consistency. How can you acquire such tools? Answer these questions:

1. *What motivates you to get up in the morning?*

2. *What do you do about it?*

Motivated Muscles Move

I look at motivation as a large muscle in the life of any thriving athlete, business professional and/or entrepreneur. It is developed and built through identifying personal goals by answering the question, *why do I do what I do?*

Take a quick inventory of what *motivates* you.

What is your purpose in life? In business? In relationships? (Go back to Chapter 1 if you need a reminder.)

What are your goals in life? In business? In relationships?

What is the *purpose* of your goals in life? In business? In relationships?

As you answer these questions, please note that *purpose* goes hand in hand with *vision*. When you understand your purpose, it's easier to cast vision and create goals toward accomplishing vision. To build muscle to go the distance, purpose and goals must be defined and fleshed out.

Watch the Clock

The next step to getting off the bench is the awareness that the clock is ticking. Time is your most limited commodity, and there are two important things to be aware of:

- *Every* **moment counts.**
- **You can't get time back.**

If you have children, you understand the saying, "Days go slowly, but moments go quickly." If you don't have kids, allow me to explain.

You tend to think you have all the time in the world to raise your kids. Then, one day, you wake up, and they're graduating from high school, college, then getting married. Time has passed, and with it, opportunities. All you have left to show for it is memories.

I hate to be the bearer of bad news, but it's the same with your dreams, your goals and your visions. As time passes, so do opportunities. Don't allow time to be the reason you don't succeed. The only way to avoid wasting time is to intentionally **not** waste time!

Since you don't have all the time in the world, linking time to your approach is **crucial**. The things that consume your time should always point back to your vision and goals.

Take a weekday in my life to illustrate my point. Many people tell me I'm insane when they see this. But I'm here to tell you that I'm not insane. I am *intentional*.

- I wake up at 3:55 AM.

- I pray and spend time with God.

- I run three miles on the high school track.

- I run bleachers.

- I lift weights.

- I shower.

At 6 AM I'm in the office and working my business until around 6 or 7 at night.

Why would I get up at 3:55 and wear myself out before going to run my business? Madness? No! I have stuff to get out of bed for! Meaningful stuff!

Here is my motivation:

- My God. He is good, and His purpose is my pursuit.

- My family. They are the beat of my heart.

- My jobs. They... What? Hold the ball!

Yes, my jobs. I love what I do! I am a business owner who prides himself on helping people. My customers know they can count on me. They trust me to work hard for them; thus I work long hours, I am dependable and I make myself available to them.

Also, I am an SEC Football Official. If I want to continue to be an SEC Football Official, I must be willing to go beyond working a 6 AM to 6 PM job. See, the difficult extras in my life are not optional. They are necessary, much like resistance is necessary to build muscle.

Note how much time I spend exercising. I could spend that time a million other ways, but nothing else would give me the return I need to accomplish what I'm trying to do. I understand that exercise is essential if I want to continue my journey in the SEC. Therefore, I spend much of my time exercising.

Acknowledging these realities keeps me motivated through mundane miles on the track and fixes my feet on the bleachers at least five times a week.

Extra Effort

I think I stated it earlier, but it fits here, too. Most of getting off the bench is about intentionality, effort and timing.   If you haven't started moving those muscles, well, now's the time! If you are already doing so, push harder. The only one who should be called off the bench is the one prepared to make the necessary play. Make sure that's **you**!

"Get on the line!"
- Coach Don Stringer

Run! Don't Walk.

Once you have the discipline to work that motivational muscle, get your cardio on. Run don't walk! If you are serious about your goals and managing your time wisely, your default in life will be to pursue things with full force.

My friend Cammie Scott likes to say, "Walk with a purpose because you could collide with destiny." With discipline, motivation and determination, my collision with destiny is well on its way to reality.

Hopefully your destiny is on its way to reality, too. Make the collision happen! You are destined to get off the bench and get in the game if you are motivated to do so!

PLAYBOOK: Get off the Bench

1. Remind yourself again, what is your purpose/vision? For your life? For your profession? For your family?

2. Define the next level and your motivation for getting there.

3. List the basic things you need to do to maintain this level.

4. List the things you need to do to get to the next level.

5. Do you need to restructure your time in order to get off the bench? If so, how?

CHAPTER 7

GET IN THE GAME

TODAY IS THE FIRST DAY OF THE REST OF YOUR LIFE

Positive coaching, casting the vision, being a team player, recognizing what motivates you and linking that to using time wisely are part of the process of acquiring field presence. What comes next?

Only In My Dreams?

From as far back as I can remember in childhood, it was my goal to be an NFL football player! I was determined and ultimately, I made a good run at it. I played semi-pro football and did pretty well. Then I tried out for several professional teams. Despite my longing and giving it my best shot, I never made the cut. I was disappointed as I watched the doors to play in the NFL close. But I didn't stay disappointed for long.

It occurred to me that my dream hadn't completely crumbled. I could still get on the field in the NFL. It was just going to look a little different from what I'd planned. My goal then turned to *officiating* in the NFL. All I needed next was the strategy to get there.

Goals are SMART, but it's better to be Booker SMAART

In the November 1981 issue of *Management Review*, George Doran, Arthur Miller, and James Cunningham coined the acronym S.M.A.R.T., in an article on improving project management processes in business. Though there are variations, the acronym stuck. Goals should be S.M.A.R.T. to create a path toward a purpose with evident indicators and an appraisal of the goal's accomplishment. I think their premise is genius. But as **Beth Snyder Jones**, my colleague from the National Association of Insurance and Financial Advisors, points out, there is a key ingredient missing: another A – Accountability.

Booker SMAART

Let's take a closer look.

Specific – Make goals specific enough to know you are actually accomplishing them! For instance, my specific goal is reaching the top level as a football official, but for now, I'm focusing on being a valuable official in the SEC. I want to be the best where I am, which will increase my options of moving up.

Think of goals as a dart board. Note the outside circles and use those to perfect your aim. When you use those to find the center of the board, every shot will get you closer to your goal – the bulls-eye.

Measureable – You need to see whether you're moving forward, so your specific goals must be assessed. This can be realized in many ways, but my favorite assessment is the most basic: who, what, when, where and how.

Who – Who is working toward the goal? It could be you, your business, your church, your team, etc.

What – What is the specific goal? Break it down. The smallest piece should point back to the main goal. For instance, don't just have an annual goal. Break it into monthly, weekly and daily goals. The daily goal should always line up with the annual goal.

When – When should this goal be completed to stay on track for your long-term objective? Does it need to be completed in few months? A week? A few days? A few hours? Right now?

Where – Where does meeting this goal put you on your way to fulfilling your dream? Will you be one year closer to your dream after meeting this goal? Will you be one class closer? Will you be one level closer? Acknowledge that you're moving closer to the goal. It helps you keep momentum.

<u>How</u> – By what manner will this goal be achieved? How will you do it? Practice? Work? Study? Exercise? Meditate? School/seminar? Specifically name what you need to do accomplish your next step.

This is extremely important. I've seen it again and again: professionals set reasonable goals, yet never achieve them. It's not because they can't; it's not because they lack expertise or education; it's simply because **they never plan how to achieve their goals.**

How to "How to"

As a coach, I created a game plan for each game. I designed plays with specific formations and specific blocking techniques. I would run one play to set up another play. Then, my next move depended on how the opposing team reacted to my last play. We could score a touchdown in one play or 15 plays depending on how well my team executed. The point is that we had a strategy which was practiced, so we knew how to accomplish our objective on the field. That's what **you** need!

How are you going to accomplish your dream? This section is where you figure it out.

84

Here are examples from my own life:

Specific Football Goal: Make it to the NFL.

Measurement:

What: I want to become an Official in the NFL.

How: I'll begin with high school officiating. Once I've made it to the top of that league, I'll aim for college officiating. Once I make it to the top of college, I'll set my eyes on the NFL.

When: Current – to be accomplished in the next two years.

Where: Since I hit my target in the high school league, I'm working on the second phase of my strategy: college football. I will continue to do my best at this level and reach for the next one.

I've been blessed, and I am extremely grateful for each step and goal achieved along this path. Though my primary goal is to make it to the NFL, for now, I'm relentlessly working to be the best in the SEC.

Specific goal in business: Make the company trip next year.

Measurement:

Who: This goal involves my staff and me.

What: We need to accrue enough points to make the company

leadership trip.

How: I need to address my customer's needs, consistently and in a

timely manner by answering phone calls or providing my cell

number so I can be reached when I'm out of the office.

I can increase client base by hosting a faculty meeting at one

new school per month.

Add ___ amount of new Property & Casualty

Add ___ amount of Life Insurance.

Add ___ amount of retirement seminars.

When: I will need to check my numbers, weekly and monthly to make

sure I stay on track. If my monthly goals remain on track, I will

make the leadership trip. If they are too low, I'll need to

reevaluate/re-work my strategy to make up what I lack.

Here is where I added an extra "A" so SMART becomes *Booker*

***SMAART*:**

Accountability – Be accountable to someone for setting and reaching

your goals. One of the most beneficial ways to stay on track is

accountability. It significantly increases the probability of successfully accomplishing your goals. The reason it works is simple: you don't want to let another person down. It is easy to say you don't want to let yourself down. However, when you invite someone to join your journey by sharing your goals and strategies, you create a relationship dynamic. In doing so, you invite challenging dialogue and questions that have to be answered.

- "What is your process to reach this goal?"
- "Do you need to reevaluate this goal? "
- "Why didn't you do something differently to reach your goal?"
- "When will we talk again about your progress?"

Such questions challenge you to be reliable and follow through on days it might be easier to make excuses.

Likewise, there is the added benefit of comradery and support. A good accountability partner will provide positive feedback and ask tough questions, but will also offer encouragement and inspiration. In turn, you can provide the same for him/her.

Attainable – Is the goal realistic for you at this time?

Is it within your power, ability and skill level? Your answer should always be yes. If it's not, you need to reevaluate your specific goal, and perhaps redefine it. For instance, when it became evident I would not make it to the NFL as a football player, I adjusted my goal so it was attainable. I'm still working to make the NFL, but now I'm working to make it as an official.

Relevant – Does the goal relate to your dream? Does it relate to your actual life?

At times, you may find a specific goal that you've listed doesn't coincide with what you hope to accomplish in the future. In such a case, working toward it becomes a waste of time and energy.

Here is an example. I started a minor league football team. Our team did well, and we did so quickly. However, the league didn't do well, so we folded.

I believed in what I was doing, and I was proud of how far we made it. It was heartbreaking to see the team, as well as all that I worked long and hard to accomplish, deteriorate before my eyes. Yet, even though I was disappointed, I didn't spend all my time figuring out how to keep the league going. That was not going to get me where I ultimately wanted to be. I invested my time in officiating because it was more relevant to my future.

Again, each specific goal should point back to your dream. Analyze whether achieving your *Booker* SMAART goals will get you closer to where you want to be, or whether they are merely a distraction.

Time-based – Your goals should be accomplished in a certain amount of time.

Keep in mind that you can err on the side of too much or too little. Too much time allotted to achieve goals leads to wasting your most valuable commodity. Too little time leads to frustration.

Take losing weight for example.

Specific health goal: Lose 15 pounds this year

Measurement:

What: 1.5 pounds per month

How: Reduce sugar intake, eat clean on 80/20 rule and exercise or do yoga for 30-60 minutes, 5 times per week

When: Current – to be accomplished by this time next year

Measureable: Weigh weekly to monitor progress

89

Attainable: 1.5 pounds per month is attainable, while 5 pounds per

month is not.

Accountable: Who will I be accountable to so that I stay on track?

Monthly or more frequent calls to check in. Celebrate

the successes.

Relevant: Is my overall health better? Do I feel a difference? Do

I feel better about myself?

Timely: Is this the right time to engage in this goal?

If I have health issues and cannot exercise or live up to the

healthy eating right now, or if my schedule does not allow for the

exercise regimen, then it is not the right time to focus on this goal.

Using my dream to play in the NFL as an example, I had a

window of time to achieve becoming an NFL player. Once I realized it

wasn't going to happen, I didn't allow myself more time to make it

because it would've been time wasted. Instead, I found another way to

get there – again, setting my goals within a time frame.

The Bowl is my Goal

In the SEC, my yearly goal is to make a Bowl Game. How do I do that?

1. I keep my work out schedule.

2. I take care of myself.

3. I stay in tune with the rules and regulations of the game.

4. I consistently make accurate calls on the field.

One success leads to another success.

If I've been the best; if I've met my goals, I'll be a contender for a Bowl Game. Consequently, if I'm picked for a Bowl Game, I am a better candidate for officiating in the NFL.

Push

> *"Remember that guy who gave up?*
> *Neither does anybody else."*

We each start at number one. The challenge is staying number one. You may have to shift some things. You may have to stretch yourself. I can almost guarantee you will have disappointments along the way. But you can succeed!   Whatever happens during your first plays of the game, keep going!   Be consistent with your Booker SMAART goals. Set the mark, create your strategy, acquire strong accountability

and then, move toward your goal.

"Today is the first day of the rest of your life."

- Coach Mike Isom

PLAYBOOK: Get in the Game

Create your own Booker SMAART inventory and strategy.

1. Create an index card with separate categories to take inventory:

Personal Life

Professional Life

Any other area you desire to focus.

You might even decide to have these listed on your smart phone and have an alarm set to remind you to look at them.

2. Use the Booker SMAART acronym for each category you listed.

Specific Goal:

Measurement:

Who:

What:

How:

When:

Where:

Accountability:

Attainability:

Realistic:

Time:

3. Evaluate each goal, at least monthly, to make sure you're on track or consider whether your goals need to be altered. If you're not on track, you will detect it early enough to adjust with little to no time lost.

4. Adjust as needed.

5. Repeat the process.

CHAPTER 8

PLAY YOUR POSITION

HIT THE HOLE RUNNING, CLEAR THE LINE AND USE YOUR GOD GIVEN TALENTS

When officiating as a field judge, part of my job is to count the number of defensive players on the field. But let's say that I become distracted because I think the umpire is standing in the wrong area, so I try to get his attention and tell him to move. The play has started, and suddenly, I hear yelling and cursing from the crowd. I look at the defensive line – where I should've been looking in the first place. It's obvious why the crowd is yelling. There are too many defensive players on the field. I missed a call.

It's Not an Option

To have field presence, playing your position is not optional; it's imperative. It is obvious that playing your position in sports is important to win a game. But in your professional life, the way you play your position can make or break your career. When you don't play it well, the foundation, which everyone worked to put into place, falters.

"Hit the hole running, clear the line and use your God given talents."

- Coach Doug Dorris

Do you understand your position? Are you cognizant of the obligations and requirements of your job? All of them? Cognizance of your position means you realize the *purpose* of your job, the *stages* of your job, *how to recognize* if something is wrong in your job,

etc. Without such awareness, it's impossible to play your position.

Be Responsible

When you think about it, everything you need to play your

position begins and ends with responsibility. Many would say, "Of

course. That's common sense." Yet, you'd be surprised by how many

people go through the motions of a job without sufficiently

understanding what they're doing. It's no wonder so many individuals

get stuck in a dead end job, or never get promoted. As it turns out,

many never get past an entry-level position because they have

sabotaged themselves by not knowing what they don't know. The

simple truth is that what you don't know can kill your potential.

A position must be clearly and consistently defined

to be properly realized.

Obviously, this includes appropriate training as well as a keen

awareness of employers' expectations. However, please notice that I am

not placing this responsibility at the feet of the employer. If you desire

good field presence, it is your responsibility to make sure you and your employer are on the same page. A solid understanding can usually be accomplished by discussing, in detail, a well-developed job description.

Within an effective job description should be opportunities for development and continued education pertinent to your role.

Embrace Boundaries

However, don't forget to *also* look for where the specifics of a position ends. Keep in mind that positions are both defined and sustained by understanding who does what and then allowing them to do their part.   A large part of learning a position is understanding boundaries – what you will be accountable for versus what is another person's responsibility.

Since everyone on the team has a position, ignoring details of who does what will undermine teamwork vital to the team's overall success.

Allow me to give you an example within the context of baseball. You don't want the catcher of a baseball game running to left field to catch a line drive. Left field is someone else's position. If the catcher leaves his responsibility at home plate to run after a line drive, who will be at home to catch the ball and tag the person running home from third? Hopefully, the third baseman? Wouldn't the defense be better if the catcher stayed home and the line drive was caught by the left-fielder? Yes! If the catcher plays his position, and the outfielder plays his, the outfielder can throw the ball to the catcher at home and stop the runner from scoring.

The Devil is in the Details

As an SEC football official, I'm expected to know the rules of the game, at all times. Every little detail matters. It is my responsibility to memorize the rules, understand them and know how to call them properly, under a lot of stress, around a lot of large men. And that's just the tip of the iceberg.

If I don't realize the enormity of my job, how can I be prepared to execute my best? All the more, if I can't trust my teammates to know the details of their job, how can I execute my best? The truth is that I can't. Nor can the team.

Become the Best

There are several excuses for not being the best at what we do.

1. Sometimes it's because of what I just explained, we don't fully understand the details of our position.

2. Sometimes it's because we want to keep moving; we want a *different* position.

Neither excuse is acceptable, especially number two. One thing I've understood the Lord telling me is that whatever position I'm in, I need to be the best! When I need a reminder to work hard despite my position, I look to the Old Testament example of King David.

King David is highly regarded as the best and most beloved king of Israel. Even more impressive, he has the honor of being deemed, "...a man after God's own heart," by God, Himself.

David was honored to be God's choice as king, replacing Saul when the time was right. However, it was only after David served his family as a simple shepherd that he was given the opportunity to serve God's people as king. Being the best shepherd was David's opportunity to show what he was made of.

When you think about it, David was definitely an over-achiever. I mean, he blew the top off that being a shepherd-thing! Notice, we never read about David losing any sheep. He must have aced that responsibility. What we read is that in his position as shepherd, he killed the Philistine giant Goliath and rescued God's people from ridicule and defeat! I ask myself, "Had David not been a shepherd, would he have been given the opportunity to show his faith and courage to those who doubted God's power? If he hadn't been a shepherd, would it be evident to the world that God could use anyone —a kid with a sling-shot and a few stones - to accomplish His goals? I think part of God's plan was to show us we can be used in miraculous ways regardless of our position.

God expects me to do my best, despite my level, despite my circumstances and despite my desires for more.

I'm giving everything I've got while I'm officiating in the SEC. That doesn't mean I forget about pursuing the next level. It means I should be my best, *regardless* of my level.

> **"Big jobs usually go to the men who prove**
> **their ability to outgrow small ones."**
> **— Ralph Waldo Emerson**

You might think, "It's great that David showed himself to be the best at the task at hand and God made him the leader of His people. But

101

things don't always turn out like that." You're right. What about the times you do the best at your position but are *not* crowned king?

At lunch one afternoon, I asked a friend this question: "Can you think of an athlete who was always the best at his position, even when it didn't benefit him to do so?" He said the same name echoing in the back of my mind: Scottie Pippen.

Scottie Pippen, a fellow graduate of the University of Central Arkansas, was one of the greatest NBA players of all time. He is the only player to win an NBA title and Olympic gold medal in the same year – **twice**! He made basketball history with fellow-player, Michael Jordan, winning six NBA championship titles.

"Well, of course," you think. "Anyone who played with Michael Jordan made history." I'll give you that. But Pippen was different. He was both a coach's dream player and a team's dream player. Why? Because despite his unbelievable talent to play almost any position on the court, he played the position he was told. Pippen competed *where* he was needed and *when* he was needed there, following instruction from his coach.

To fully understand what I'm saying, look at Pippen's category assists. They total over 6,000! That number screams, "I'm the BEST!" Yet there is something more important to note. The category is career *assists*. Pippen didn't make those shots; he assisted his teammates in making them. When I realized that, my perspective changed from being impressed with Pippen's individual talent to being impressed by his team-player mentality and his discipline to focus on his team above all else. That's how it's done!

Pippen played his position and pushed to attain the vision of the team, time after time, win after win. Without his dedication to play his position, I'm not sure as many wins would've been possible.

When each member of the team knows his or her job, takes responsibility for his or her position, plays his or her best and executes consistently, field presence is at its peak. Winning then becomes a byproduct of the hard work put forth by every position on the entire team.

Translating that to life field presence, when you take responsibility for your position, play your best and do so consistently, everyone benefits. Individuals, teams, businesses, churches, families, etc. Many times, the outcome of such field presence is more responsibility, more room to grow, more ways to inspire and ultimately, more field presence.

PLAYBOOK: Play your Position

1.   What does play your position mean in your job?

2.   As a coach, do you encourage your players to play their
      position, or do you coach as though you don't care who gets it
      done as long as it gets done? What are the pros and cons to the
      different approaches?

3.   Identify what you need to better play your position.

4.   Scottie Pippen could play any position on the court, but he
      limited himself to the position his team needed him to play. By
      doing so, his team won championships, but he didn't always get
      the credit he deserved. (Most of the time, Michael Jordan got
      the credit). Are you willing to do that for your team? Why or
      why not?

CHAPTER 9

ADJUST THE PLAY

GET YOUR EDUCATION AND YOU CAN ALWAYS FALL BACK ON IT IF YOU DON'T MAKE IT TO THE NFL

First, it was arithmetic, then subject-verb agreement, scientific method, compounds and minerals, drama, history, and all the other relentless school lessons. (Yikes! Bring on the tackles and sprints!) However, in hindsight, it's a good thing that I took studying seriously, since my childhood dreams to become an NFL player never worked out.

What happens when your dreams or your goals don't culminate? I hope you've considered that possibility. Although I knew what I wanted to do from age eight, I also knew many things could happen to prevent me from accomplishing my great ambitions. My mom always told me to get my education because if football never panned out, I could always fall back on it.

> **"Get your education and you can always fall back on it if you don't make it to the NFL."**
> **- Ezelma Booker**

There are moments in the game when you realize your strategy to get the ball to the goal isn't going to work. At that point, your team has two options: continue the strategy that is not working and pray for a miracle, or change your strategy to give you a better chance. It's a no-brainer. You change the strategy. You adjust the play.

Omaha

The time was running out. The ball needed to be snapped right away, but it was obvious the strategy in play was not going to work because the defense was solid. Suddenly, the ball was snapped, and without delay, Peyton Manning shouted, "Omaha!" The offense shifted, the ball was thrown and the rest is history.

Well, history repeated itself with 56 game winning drives, currently the most of all time. Manning used his "Omaha" call quite a bit and was able to keep its meaning secret for years.

After retiring (and interviewers pestering him) Peyton Manning finally offered an explanation for "Omaha." It was an *indicator* word. It let the offense know the quarterback was changing the play. In other words, they were switching their strategy and going to Plan B. What a great plan for football and life.

Adjust to Win

Sports teams adjust the play all the time. We might not even notice it because we take it for granted, understanding that changing things up is just part of playing the game.

Consider this scenario, for instance:

The last few minutes are ticking on the game clock. Team A wants a touchdown to secure their win, but their chances of attaining that goal are dwindling. Realizing they can't make a *touchdown*, they accept their loss, pack up their gear, and go home...right? No!

They adjust. Their goal of a touchdown isn't going to happen so they look to score another way. Perhaps they go for a field goal instead of a touchdown. But one thing is certain: they don't give up a win just because their first plan didn't make it happen.

Life often calls for the same type of adjustments. There are going to be situations in your job, your family and your world when things shift quickly and you're going to have to be ready to adjust the play for the touchdown, or perhaps even look to score another way to win. Successful adjustment in life depends on the same two things as in football:

1. Know when to make the call.
2. Have a Plan B in place.

When I realized my dream of playing football in the NFL wasn't going to happen, I called "Omaha!" I changed the play. I went to my backup plan and started moving forward. As a matter of fact, the back-up plan – my Plan B – is currently in motion.

Like I explained earlier, I've still got my eye set on being on the field in the NFL. But now I'm working at it from a different angle. I am working and training to officiate in the National Football League. It will still be a BIG win!

Yearn to Learn

> *"Don't ever stop learning; for the world*
> *will never stop changing."*
> *- Anonymous*

Part of being able to adjust is having the knowledge it takes to adjust. Videos, seminars, books, podcasts – we live in a technological world, to say the least. Don't stop learning just because you are no longer required to learn. Information and education are literally at your fingertips. Learn all you can. Educate yourself about your goals, your options and your competition. The more you know, the more doors are open to you.

Lead and Follow

When adjustment is necessary, so is leadership. In my illustration earlier, the offensive line depended on their quarterback, Peyton Manning, to make the best call. Their job was to be prepared for whatever call was made and carry through. So, when adjustments are necessary, who is the offensive line and who is the quarterback?

You! There will be times you call the plays. Other times you will be making the play happen.

Set the Standard

> *"Setting an example is not the main means of influencing others, it is the only means."*
> *- Albert Einstein*

A good leader has strong work ethic. Without work ethic, influence is limited because followers don't perceive that you believe in the work you're asking them to do. If you work hard, those on your team are more likely to put forth the effort to get the job done and to do their job well.

And let's not forget credibility. If you're leading a team, you have to say what you do, do what you say and do so consistently. Don't make promises you don't intend to keep.

Furthermore, don't ask your team to do anything you're not willing to do yourself. Your followers are not there to do the jobs you dislike. They are there to help achieve a specific goal.

"What you are speaks so loudly, I can't hear what you are saying."

- Ralph Waldo Emerson

Create a Positive Culture

Good leaders also emulate the behavior they want from those who follow them. Actions like speaking to others with respect, treating others with kindness and working with integrity define the type of behavior that a leader will receive in return.

If you want to see this in action, watch how young children interact with one another. Listen closely and you will hear them say things they've consistently been told including, "No, no. Not nice. Say please..." You might even hear them drop a bad word or two, not knowing any better. They copy what they see and hear from those who lead them – their parents, older siblings or guardians.

Teams are not much different. If you want to promote resentment and blame, show your team resentment and blame (and watch everything crumble). If you want to promote camaraderie, encouragement and respect, act like it.

Create a culture of kindness and optimism by the way you treat others. More often than not, your team will follow your lead, creating the same positive atmosphere down the line.

Leader or Follower?

Sometimes the play on the field dictates who leads and who follows. Understanding what is required at any given time empowers you to take the cue and make the play happen as a QB or as part of the offensive line. Either way, your ultimate job is to mobilize the team, communicate the message and put words into action. The goal is your willingness to adjust the play as necessary for the win.

Adjusting the play is a difficult part of field presence because it requires a player to adjust yet still make good decisions and do both quickly. In football, this takes a lot of practice. In life, it takes a lot of

planning and a lot of prayer.

PLAYBOOK: Adjust the Play

1. What is an "Omaha" play?

2. Why is an "Omaha" important?

3. Do you have a Plan B? If not, spend time creating one. Keep in mind that you don't have to abandon your dream or your goal. You might simply need to adjust the play.

4. What does leadership have to do with adjusting the play?

CHAPTER 10

NEVER QUIT

IF YOU FALL, FALL FORWARD

"Success is to be measured not so much by the position that one has reached in life as by the obstacles which have been overcome while trying to succeed."
— *Booker T. Washington*

Here I am. I have written this book about how field presence is more than showing up at the game and taking a position on the field. It's even more than merely getting out there and giving it your best shot.

- It's more than looking a specific way.

- It's more than being confident.

- It's more than achieving a goal.

- It's more than being mediocre.

- It's more than being satisfied.

- It's more than fighting over who is going to lead and who is going to follow.

Life field presence is the physical and mental ability for a person to see and respond in the right way at just the right time, despite distractions. It is intentional and once acquired and applied, you reap the benefits of having the reputation as one who has it.

As wonderful as all that is, here at the end, I have some unsettling news: You can have field presence, galore, and *still* lose the game.

It happens all the time. You show up with the team, get off the bench, get into the game and look the part. You can be the best at your position, have confidence, command respect and adjust as necessary, but still lose. It's a bummer.

"If you fall, fall forward."
- Coach Clifton Ealy

So what do you do if (or when) you lose? All I can say is, "Playing the game in the face of losing gets you ready for the game you're going to win…" But only if you **don't quit**!

Choose Future Not Failure

Remember how we started this journey. I opened with examples of well-known individuals who failed – successful people from different eras, different backgrounds, different educations and different careers.

Think about Albert Einstein. He is the guy renowned for his intelligence to the point that his name is now equated with genius. Have you heard about his failures? He was so bad that his father died believing his son was a complete loser who would amount to nothing.

That's not all. While in college, Einstein skipped classes and considered dropping out of college altogether. His professors thought he was a terrible student who had no future. Consequently, he couldn't find and keep employment to support his family, so he lost his wife and children. Terrible son, lousy student, undependable husband and father – yet that's not the Einstein we know now, is it?

We celebrate Einstein's *achievements*, which just happened to reshape the scientific thinking of the *entire world*! You know, the theory of relativity and understanding the force of gravity. Those were *his* wins.

He could've quit. I'm sure that at times he contemplated it. But he didn't. The world is better because Einstein chose his future rather than choosing failure. Ultimately, I believe enduring his failures led Einstein to his collision with destiny.

The same can be true of you.

119

"It's hard to beat a person who never gives up."

-Babe Ruth

Perhaps you remember the British athlete Derek Redmond from the 1992 Olympic Games in Barcelona, Spain. He was a major contender for the gold medal in the 400 meters relay, but he never made it to the final race. Devastatingly, Redmond's hamstring tore during the semifinal 400, destroying his chance to continue to compete for the gold on behalf of Great Britain. Ultimately, Redmond was recorded in the 1992 Olympic records as "Did Not Finish" the event. Yet history remembers Derek Redmond for the opposite. The way he finished became one of the most extraordinary Olympic stories of all time.

The world watched as Redmond collapsed in distress about 250 meters from the finish line. He was literally writhing on the ground in agony. Stretchers were provided to carry him off the field, but he refused them. He stood, screaming in pain, and staggered toward the end. His father, fighting the crowd and security guards, made his way to his son, helped him stand, and together, they faced the goal. Heartbroken but determined, Redmond crossed the finish line with the help of his dad, along with the standing ovation of 65,000 spectators.

No Excuses

There is no doubt that everyone who witnessed Redmond's finish was inspired. After all, Redmond had an easy way off that field – a stretcher. Not to mention, he had an excellent excuse to use the stretcher since he couldn't walk. However, he pushed himself to accomplish the task at hand, despite the odds, the pain and the loss, even when he didn't have to!

> *"Nothing is impossible,*
> *the word itself says, "I'm possible!"*
> *- Audrey Hepburn*

The Proverbial Achilles' heel

I had two games in one week. My first game was a nationally televised game on a Thursday night. It was rainy, with mud two inches thick! To make matters worse, I was sick the night before with food poisoning, so I was already weary from being up all night. Nevertheless, I managed to nail the game on national TV that day!

Fortunately, the next morning I felt good enough that I drove to the second game I was to officiate. It was a busy week, but I was doing what I loved, so I didn't mind.

The next day was the next game. I stretched and warmed up, just like always. The first half came and went, but during the third quarter, I felt the most excruciating pain I had ever known.

I was backpedaling on a normal, routine play. I ran in toward the players and suddenly heard what sounded like a gun shot. It felt like someone hit me with a baseball bat, knocking my ankle from where it was attached to my leg. I looked down and my foot was literally flopping as I was running. I screamed and fell, thinking I had broken my ankle. As it turns out, I had shredded my Achilles' tendon.

"Difficulties mastered are opportunities won."

- Winston Churchill

Trainers and my supervisor, Harold Mitchell, ran on the field as I tried to get up and run. "Tape it," I ordered. "I can finish the game." Ignoring me, they carried me off the field, explaining they could actually see where the Achilles had shredded. They said I was done, no discussion. I started sobbing. I couldn't help it. The tear was so severe

---

that it was obvious to everyone there that it could be the end of my career as an official.

They wrapped my achilles and gave me crutches. I sat in the escort van and watched my teammates finish the game. Once I got back to the hotel, I drove myself home.

Once home, I called my team doctor from my college football days. He fit me in and performed surgery to repair the shredded Achilles. He told me that he literally had to weave it back together. I was ordered to wear a boot for six weeks. That meant no walking and no driving. I had to stay completely off my feet. The prognosis was straightforward and bleak: my achilles would either heal or need to be repaired again. It was possible that it would be messed up the rest of my life.

Needless to say, I missed the rest of that season plus a potential bowl game that year. To add insult to injury, I received a call to be an official in the Arena Football League, while I was down. I had to decline that opportunity, since I was still in pretty bad shape.

I could not exercise or put any weight on my foot. I couldn't officiate, I couldn't work and I was worried about the money I was losing and the time this injury was taking from me. All I did was watch football and sleep, angry that I wasn't on the field doing what I loved. I slipped into depression and started gaining weight – both things I couldn't afford to do.

As I piled on the pounds, it dawned on me that I was stuck. I couldn't work out, nor could I run to get control of my weight. Fortunately, I found a work out regimen which didn't require me to be on my feet. As I worked through it consistently, my pounds began to dwindle. However, that wasn't enough to keep my cardio where it needed to be.

Though discouraged, I continued to follow the doctor's orders and the good Lord healed my achilles. Actually, it healed so well that I didn't even have to go to physical therapy!

The following year, I started over. I started running. One mile, then one and one half, then two. The rest is history. I'm now officiating and working without any issues.

Even more exciting, I'm still pursuing my dream of working in the NFL!

Be an Overcomer

Don't quit! Part of having field presence is
perseverance. Overcome whatever gets in your way. Don't let anything,
even legitimate things, stop you from accomplishing your goal or your
dream.

> *Your only guarantee on the field*
> *is if you quit, you lose.*

You may have to adjust. You might not win the gold. You may
have to work longer and harder to make it.   Ultimately, your field
presence might look different than you anticipated, like Redmond's. But
you'll never have field presence if you quit.

PLAYBOOK: Don't Quit

1. Have you ever allowed your failures to overshadow your successes? If so, how? If not, why?

2. What are some excuses or circumstances keeping you from achieving your full potential?

3. Are the excuses listed for question 2 worth giving up your dream? Why or why not?

4. Does your goal or dream need to be adjusted to keep you from quitting?

5. What if field presence looks different than you anticipated?

CHAPTER 11

FIELD PRESENCE -
IT'S MORE THAN JUST PLAYING THE GAME

IT'S NOT THE SIZE OF THE DOG IN THE FIGHT, IT'S THE SIZE OF THE FIGHT IN THE DOG

When we started this journey together, we acknowledged that field presence is a term primarily used in sports to describe a powerful skill and the strong demeanor of a player. Players with field presence exhibit self-control, leadership skills, command respect, and persevere, distinguishing them from others on the field. We took the same principles of field presence from the context of sports and applied them to life to use, on an intentional basis.

Everyday life has its challenges. Career challenges, family challenges, political challenges, community challenges and the list goes on. To put it in sports terms, we are all faced with tackles, jukes, resistance, fouls, sacks, disappointments, failures, even brokenness. As we discussed in Chapter 10, we all lose at some point! However, win or lose, by applying field presence to your life, you acquire qualities which move you forward. You gain focus, confidence, diligence, courage, motivation, leadership strategies and more.

I am not going to lie. Having field presence requires a lot of hard work! I wasn't kidding when I said, "It's more than just playing the game!" But using these principles got me through some of my biggest failures. Moreover, as I *continue* to apply them to my life, I *continue* to experience success. It's not just possible, it's probable that you will experience success, too!   The words of **Coach Charles Vereen** still echo in my ears: **"It's not the size of the dog in the fight, it's the size of the fight in the dog!"**

Be encouraged! Stay with it. Remember your *why*, remember it's worth the work and remember to focus on where you want to be. Intentionally apply the principles for Field Presence to your life. After all, it's *really* not enough to just play the game. You also have to *earn your stripes.* I write about how in my next book, named that very thing - *Earn your Stripes.*

*Many thanks to my friends and associates for your
kind words and encouragement! You continue to inspire me.*

"I've always liked Wes because when I first met him, I knew he was a humble man with a great heart for serving others." **Anthony Lucas, Former player for Razorbacks**

"I really enjoyed playing football under Wes' leadership as head coach. The best I've had but also a great man that always put God first. I'm proud and honored to call him my friend. May God continue to bless you in all you do." **Cedric Williams, #35 Rhinos football player**

"To my great friend. Congrats and thanks for always being yourself." **Anthony Jeffries, #36 NFL Field Judge**

"Wes Booker is an engaging leader with passion and energy. I am proud to call him a friend, a colleague and an inspiration."

John T. Murphy CPCU, API
Region Executive
The Horace Mann Companies

"Wes is a highly skilled football official who has an instinctive knack for the game… He is also a genuinely great person who always puts others before himself."

Byron Hatch
SEC Assistant Commissioner for Competition/Championships

"Wes and I have been friends for over 20 years. I've watched him pursue God as well as his goals without being deterred. Many will be blessed by reading his story." **Robert Upshaw, Upshaw Ministries**